Empowered

Boundaries

A Guided Journal To Self Healing And Authentic Living

SUCCESS PUBLICATIONS

DESCRIPTION

This book is a transformative tool designed to help you reconnect with your true self and embark on a journey of deep healing and genuine living. This journal provides a safe space for self-exploration, reflection, and growth, empowering you to heal past wounds and embrace your authentic identity.

You'll get;

- Healing Exercises: Practical activities and techniques to facilitate emotional healing and personal growth.

- Reflective Prompts: Insightful questions to help you uncover your true desires, values, and strengths.

- Mindfulness Practices: Tools to cultivate awareness, presence, and inner peace in your daily life.

- Inspirational Quotes: Words of wisdom to motivate and guide you on your journey towards authenticity.

- Personal Growth Plans: Frameworks to set meaningful goals, track your progress, and celebrate your achievements.

This book is more than just a journal; it's a supportive guide on your path to self-discovery and healing. Whether you're overcoming past traumas, seeking greater self-awareness, or striving to live more authentically, this journal offers the guidance and inspiration you need. Embrace your journey with compassion and courage, and let "Authentic You" help you live a life true to yourself.

CHAPTER 1: UNDERSTANDING BOUNDARIES

Boundaries are a crucial aspect of mental and emotional health, serving as the invisible lines that define where one person ends and another begins. Establishing and maintaining healthy boundaries is vital for personal well-being, relationships, and overall life satisfaction. This chapter delves into the fundamental concepts of boundaries, their importance, and how to identify your own personal boundaries.

Subtopic 1: What Are Boundaries?

Definition and Importance

Boundaries are the limits and rules we set for ourselves within relationships. They delineate where our physical space, emotions, and responsibilities end and where those of others begin. Boundaries are essential because they:

1. Protect our emotional well-being: By establishing what is acceptable and unacceptable behaviour, boundaries help protect us from emotional harm.

2. Define our identity: Boundaries make it clear what we value, believe, and prioritize.

3. Enhance relationships: Healthy boundaries foster mutual respect and understanding in relationships.

4. Promote self-respect: By setting boundaries, we demonstrate self-respect and demand the same from others.

Types of Boundaries

Understanding the different types of boundaries can help us identify where we need to set limits in various aspects of our lives. The primary types of boundaries include:

1. Physical Boundaries: These pertain to personal space and physical touch. For example, deciding who can touch you and how close others can get to you.

2. Emotional Boundaries: These involve separating your emotions from others. It includes not taking on the emotions or issues of others and protecting yourself from emotional manipulation.

3. Mental Boundaries: These refer to your thoughts, opinions, and values. They involve having your own beliefs and respecting others' beliefs without forcing yours on them.

4. Spiritual Boundaries: These pertain to your faith, spirituality, and religious beliefs. They involve respecting your own and others' spiritual beliefs and practices.

Subtopic 2: Identifying Personal Boundaries

Reflecting on Past Experiences

One of the most effective ways to identify personal boundaries is to reflect on past experiences where you felt uncomfortable, disrespected, or violated. Consider the following reflective questions:

- When did I feel my space or privacy was invaded?

- When did I feel emotionally drained after an interaction?

- When did I compromise my beliefs to please others?

These reflections can highlight areas where boundaries were crossed and need to be reinforced.

Recognizing Boundary Breaches

Recognizing when your boundaries have been breached is critical to setting and maintaining them. Common signs of boundary violations include:

- Feeling resentment or anger: This often indicates that your boundaries are being crossed.

- Feeling exhausted or overwhelmed: Consistently feeling this way after interactions can be a sign that your emotional boundaries are not being respected.

- Avoiding certain people or situations: This can be a coping mechanism for unaddressed boundary violations.

Prompts and Exercises for Chapter 1

Prompts

1. "Describe a time when you felt your boundaries were respected. How did it make you feel?"

   - Reflect on an instance where your boundaries were honored. How did the person respect your limits? How did it impact your relationship with them?

2. "What are some situations in which you feel your boundaries are often crossed?"

   - Identify specific scenarios where you frequently feel uncomfortable or disrespected. How do these situations affect you emotionally and mentally?

3. "List three personal boundaries you have. Are these boundaries currently being respected by the people in your life?"

   - Consider your existing boundaries in various aspects of your life. Assess whether these boundaries are upheld by those around you.

Exercises

1. Boundary Mapping Exercise

   - Draw a boundary map of your life. Create sections for different areas such as work, family, friends, and self-care. Label each section with boundaries you have or need to establish. Use colors or symbols to indicate boundaries that feel strong and those that need reinforcement.

2. Boundary Reflection Journal

   - Start a boundary reflection journal. Each day, write about any situations where you felt your boundaries were tested or crossed. Reflect on how you responded and what you could do differently in the future.

3. Boundary Visualization Exercise

   - Practice a visualization exercise to strengthen your boundaries. Close your eyes and imagine a protective barrier around you. Visualize this barrier as strong and impenetrable, allowing you to interact with others without compromising your well-being. Reflect on how this visualization makes you feel.

4. Mindfulness Meditation for Boundaries

 - Engage in a 5-minute mindfulness meditation focused on boundaries. Sit comfortably, close your eyes, and take deep breaths. As you breathe in, imagine your boundaries becoming clearer and stronger. As you exhale, release any tension or fear related to boundary setting. Journal your thoughts and feelings after the meditation.

 Conclusion

Understanding boundaries is the first step toward empowered living. By recognizing the different types of boundaries and reflecting on past experiences, we can identify where our limits lie and how to assert them effectively. This chapter sets the foundation for exploring deeper aspects of boundary setting and maintenance in the subsequent chapters. Through prompts and exercises, you will begin to gain clarity on your personal boundaries and develop the confidence to uphold them in all areas of your life.

ENTER YOUR JOURNAL HERE

CHAPTER 2: SELF-AWARENESS AND SELF-REFLECTION

Self-awareness and self-reflection are foundational practices for setting and maintaining healthy boundaries. They involve a deep understanding of oneself, including personal needs, values, emotions, and limits. By cultivating self-awareness and engaging in regular self-reflection, individuals can better identify and assert their boundaries, leading to a more authentic and empowered life.

Subtopic 1: Self-Awareness

Importance of Knowing Yourself

Self-awareness is the conscious knowledge of one's own character, feelings, motives, and desires. It is crucial for boundary setting because:

1. Clarifies Personal Needs: Knowing what you need helps you establish boundaries that protect those needs.

2. Informs Decision-Making: Self-awareness aids in making decisions that align with your values and well-being.

3. Enhances Emotional Regulation: Understanding your emotional triggers allows you to manage them effectively and communicate your boundaries calmly.

4. Improves Relationships: Being aware of your own needs and limits enables you to communicate them clearly, fostering healthier relationships.

Recognizing Personal Needs and Limits

To set effective boundaries, you need to recognize your personal needs and limits. Consider these steps:

1. Identify Core Values: Reflect on what is most important to you. Your values can guide your boundary-setting process.

2. Acknowledge Your Emotions: Pay attention to your emotional responses in different situations. Emotions like anger, frustration, and discomfort often signal that a boundary is needed or has been crossed.

3. Assess Physical and Mental Limits: Understand your physical and mental capacity. Recognize when you need rest, space, or time alone.

4. Understand Relationship Dynamics: Reflect on how different relationships affect you. Identify interactions that uplift you versus those that drain you.

Subtopic 2: Reflective Practices

Journaling Techniques

Journaling is a powerful tool for self-reflection and self-awareness. It allows you to process your thoughts and emotions, gain insights into your behavior, and track your progress in boundary setting. Here are some effective journaling techniques:

1. Stream-of-Consciousness Writing: Write continuously for a set period without worrying about grammar or structure. This helps uncover subconscious thoughts and feelings.

2. Prompt-Based Journaling: Use specific prompts to guide your writing and explore particular aspects of your life and boundaries.

3. Gratitude Journaling: Regularly noting what you are grateful for can enhance your overall well-being and highlight areas where you need stronger boundaries to protect your positive experiences.

4. Reflective Journaling: After significant events or interactions, write about what happened, how you felt, and what boundaries you might need to set or reinforce as a result.

Meditation and Mindfulness

Meditation and mindfulness practices are essential for developing self-awareness and maintaining a calm, centered state of mind. These practices can help you become more attuned to your needs and boundaries. Here are some methods to incorporate into your routine:

1. Mindfulness Meditation: Sit quietly and focus on your breath, bringing your attention back whenever it wanders. This practice helps you stay present and aware of your internal states.

2. Body Scan Meditation: Lie down and mentally scan your body from head to toe, noting any areas of tension or discomfort. This can help you identify physical boundaries that need attention.

3. Loving-Kindness Meditation: Focus on sending positive thoughts to yourself and others. This practice can strengthen emotional boundaries by promoting compassion and understanding without sacrificing your own needs.

4. Guided Visualization: Imagine scenarios where you successfully set and maintain boundaries. Visualizing positive outcomes can build confidence and preparedness.

Prompts and Exercises for Chapter 2

Prompts

1. "List three personal needs that you feel are not being met currently. How can you address them?"

   - Identify unmet needs in your life. Reflect on steps you can take to meet these needs, whether through setting new boundaries or reinforcing existing ones.

2. "Write about a recent experience where you felt overwhelmed. What boundary could you have set to prevent this feeling?"

   - Analyze a situation where you felt overwhelmed and consider what boundary might have helped you manage the situation better.

3. "Describe a time when you compromised your values. How did it make you feel, and what boundary could you set to prevent this in the future?"

   - Reflect on an experience where you went against your values. Think about the emotions it triggered and how setting a boundary could protect your values moving forward.

Exercises

1. Self-Awareness Inventory

   - Create a comprehensive inventory of your values, needs, and limits. Divide your inventory into categories such as physical, emotional, mental, and spiritual. Regularly review and update this inventory to stay in tune with yourself.

2. Daily Reflection Practice

  - Set aside time each day to reflect on your experiences. Use a journal to write about your interactions, noting any boundary-related issues. This daily practice can help you become more aware of patterns and areas for improvement.

3. Mindfulness Meditation Routine

  - Establish a daily mindfulness meditation routine. Begin with short sessions and gradually increase the duration. Use this time to tune into your inner state, recognize your needs, and visualize setting healthy boundaries.

4. Value Clarification Exercise

  - List your top ten personal values. For each value, write a brief explanation of why it is important to you. Reflect on how these values influence your boundaries and decision-making processes.

Conclusion

Self-awareness and self-reflection are essential components of empowered living and effective boundary setting. By understanding your personal needs, values, emotions, and limits, you can set boundaries that protect your well-being and foster healthier relationships. Through journaling, meditation, and mindfulness practices, you can deepen your self-awareness and enhance your ability to maintain boundaries. This chapter lays the groundwork for exploring how to establish, communicate, and uphold boundaries in various areas of your life in the following chapters.

Chapter 3: Establishing Boundaries

Establishing boundaries is a proactive step in protecting your well-being and fostering healthy relationships. It involves clearly defining your limits, communicating them effectively, and overcoming any internal obstacles such as guilt or fear. This chapter will guide you through the process of setting healthy boundaries, offering strategies and exercises to build your confidence in asserting them.

Subtopic 1: Setting Healthy Boundaries

Steps to Define Boundaries

1. Self-Assessment: Begin by assessing your needs, values, and limits. Reflect on areas in your life where you feel discomfort or resentment, as these feelings often indicate where boundaries are needed.

2. Identify Specific Boundaries: Clearly define what you are comfortable with and what you are not. For example, you might need to set limits on how much time you spend on work-related tasks outside of office hours or how you want to be treated in personal relationships.

3. Be Clear and Specific: When setting boundaries, be as specific as possible. Vague boundaries are harder to enforce. For example, instead of saying, "I need more personal time," say, "I need one hour of uninterrupted time each evening."

4. Write Them Down: Documenting your boundaries can help you clarify them and commit to upholding them. It also provides a reference point if you need to revisit them.

Communicating Boundaries Clearly

1. Choose the Right Time: Discuss boundaries in a calm, private setting. Avoid bringing them up during conflicts or high-stress situations.

2. Use "I" Statements: Frame your boundaries in terms of your own needs and feelings to avoid sounding accusatory. For example, "I need time alone to recharge after work" is more effective than "You always bother me when I get home."

3. Be Firm but Kind: Assert your boundaries confidently but with respect and kindness. This approach helps maintain relationships while ensuring your needs are met.

4. Practice Active Listening: After stating your boundaries, listen to the other person's response. Acknowledge their feelings and work towards a mutually respectful understanding.

Subtopic 2: Overcoming Guilt and Fear

Addressing Emotional Barriers

Setting boundaries can trigger feelings of guilt or fear, especially if you are not used to asserting your needs. These emotions are common but can be managed with practice and self-compassion.

1. Recognize Your Right to Boundaries: Understand that setting boundaries is a form of self-respect and self-care. You have a right to protect your well-being.

2. Challenge Negative Beliefs: Identify any negative beliefs you hold about setting boundaries, such as "I'm being selfish" or "People won't like me." Replace these with positive affirmations like "Setting boundaries is necessary for my well-being."

3. Seek Support: Talk to friends, family, or a therapist about your feelings. Support from others can validate your need for boundaries and provide encouragement.

Building Confidence in Boundary Setting

1. Start Small: Begin by setting small, manageable boundaries in low-stakes situations. This can help build your confidence and demonstrate the benefits of boundary setting.

2. Practice Self-Compassion: Be kind to yourself as you navigate the challenges of setting boundaries. Acknowledge that it is a learning process and that mistakes are part of growth.

3. Visualize Success: Regularly visualize yourself setting and maintaining boundaries confidently. This mental practice can increase your readiness to do so in real-life situations.

Prompts and Exercises for Chapter 3

Prompts

1. "Write a letter to someone explaining a boundary you need to set with them. You don't have to send it."

  - This exercise allows you to articulate your boundary in a safe space. It can help clarify your thoughts and prepare you for the actual conversation.

2. "Think of a recent situation where you felt your boundaries were not respected. How did you respond, and how could you have handled it differently?"

  - Reflecting on past experiences can provide insights into how you can improve your boundary-setting skills.

3. "List three boundaries you want to establish in your personal or professional life. What steps will you take to communicate and enforce these boundaries?"

   - Identifying specific boundaries and planning their implementation can increase your likelihood of success.

 Exercises

1. Role-Playing Scenarios

   - Practice boundary-setting scenarios with a friend or in front of a mirror. Role-playing can help you rehearse your words and build confidence in your delivery.

2. Boundary Visualization Exercise

   - Spend a few minutes each day visualizing yourself setting boundaries in various situations. Picture the positive outcomes and how you feel afterwards. This can reinforce your resolve and reduce anxiety.

3. Affirmation Writing

 - Write down positive affirmations related to boundary setting, such as "I deserve to have my needs respected" or "Setting boundaries is a sign of strength." Repeat these affirmations daily to boost your confidence.

4. Boundary-Setting Journal

 - Keep a journal dedicated to your boundary-setting journey. Record your experiences, challenges, successes, and reflections. Reviewing your progress can provide motivation and insights.

Conclusion

Establishing boundaries is a crucial step toward empowered living and self-care. By defining your needs, communicating them clearly, and overcoming emotional barriers, you can set boundaries that protect your well-being and enhance your relationships. The strategies, prompts, and exercises in this chapter provide practical tools to help you develop and assert healthy boundaries confidently. As you continue your journey, remember that setting boundaries is an ongoing process that requires self-awareness, practice, and self-compassion.

ENTER YOUR JOURNAL HERE

…………………………………………………………………………………………………

…………………………………………………………………………………………………

…………………………………………………………………………………………………

…………………………………………………………………………………………………

………………………………………………

…………………………………………………………………………………………………

…………………………………………………………………………………………………

…………………………………………………………………………………………………

CHAPTER 4: MAINTAINING BOUNDARIES

Establishing boundaries is an essential first step, but maintaining them is where the real work lies. It requires ongoing vigilance, self-awareness, and reinforcement. This chapter explores strategies for consistently upholding your boundaries, handling boundary violations effectively, and practicing self-care to support your efforts.

Subtopic 1: Consistency and Reinforcement

Importance of Consistency

Consistency in maintaining boundaries is crucial for several reasons:

1. Builds Trust: Consistently upheld boundaries foster trust in relationships. Others learn what to expect from you and respect your limits.

2. Strengthens Self-Respect: Regularly enforcing your boundaries reinforces your commitment to self-respect and self-care.

3. Reduces Confusion: Inconsistent boundaries can confuse others about your needs and limits, leading to repeated boundary violations.

Techniques for Reinforcement

1. Regular Self-Check-Ins: Periodically evaluate your boundaries and how well they are being maintained. Reflect on any situations where you felt uncomfortable or disrespected and consider adjustments as needed.

2. Clear Communication: Continuously communicate your boundaries to others. Remind people of your limits when necessary and provide gentle but firm reminders if they overstep.

3. Positive Reinforcement: Acknowledge and appreciate when others respect your boundaries. Positive reinforcement can encourage them to continue honoring your limits.

4. Assertiveness Training: Practice assertiveness in everyday interactions. Role-playing and assertiveness exercises can help you maintain your boundaries with confidence and clarity.

Creating Boundary Rituals

Incorporating rituals into your routine can reinforce your boundaries and make them a natural part of your life. Some ideas include:

1. Morning Affirmations: Start your day with affirmations that reinforce your commitment to maintaining boundaries, such as "I am worthy of respect" and "I will uphold my boundaries today."

2. End-of-Day Reflection: Spend a few minutes each evening reflecting on how well you maintained your boundaries throughout the day. Consider what went well and what could be improved.

3. Weekly Boundary Review: Set aside time each week to review your boundaries. Reflect on any challenges you faced, celebrate your successes, and plan for any necessary adjustments.

Subtopic 2: Handling Boundary Violations

Strategies to Address Violations

1. Immediate Response: When a boundary is crossed, address it as soon as possible. Calmly and clearly communicate that a boundary has been violated and state what needs to change.

2. Use "I" Statements: Express how the boundary violation affected you using "I" statements. For example, "I feel disrespected when my privacy is not respected" rather than "You always invade my privacy."

3. Set Consequences: Define and communicate consequences for repeated boundary violations. Ensure the consequences are reasonable and enforce them consistently.

4. Seek Resolution: Aim for a constructive resolution that acknowledges your boundaries and respects the other person's perspective. Open, respectful dialogue can help prevent future violations.

Self-Care After a Boundary Breach

1. Acknowledge Your Feelings: Allow yourself to feel any emotions that arise from a boundary violation. Validate your feelings and avoid self-blame.

2. Practice Self-Compassion: Be kind to yourself. Recognize that maintaining boundaries is challenging and that it's okay to experience setbacks.

3. Engage in Restorative Activities: Participate in activities that restore your sense of well-being, such as exercise, meditation, spending time in nature, or engaging in hobbies.

4. Reflect and Learn: Reflect on the boundary breach to understand what happened and how you can strengthen your boundaries moving forward. Consider whether any adjustments are needed.

Prompts and Exercises for Chapter 4

Prompts

1. "Recall a time when your boundary was violated. How did you handle it? What could you do differently next time?"

   - Reflect on a past boundary breach and consider alternative strategies for handling similar situations in the future.

2. "What are some common challenges you face in maintaining your boundaries? How can you address these challenges?"

   - Identify specific obstacles to maintaining your boundaries and brainstorm practical solutions.

3. "Describe a situation where you successfully maintained your boundary. What strategies did you use, and how did it make you feel?"

   - Reflect on a positive experience with boundary maintenance to reinforce effective strategies and boost your confidence.

Exercises

1. Boundary Reinforcement Plan

   - Develop a detailed plan for maintaining your boundaries. Outline specific strategies, rituals, and communication techniques you will use. Review and adjust the plan regularly to ensure it remains effective.

2. Role-Playing Boundary Violations

   - Practice handling boundary violations through role-playing exercises. Enlist a friend or family member to help simulate various scenarios. Focus on using clear communication, assertiveness, and setting consequences.

3. Self-Care Toolkit

   - Create a self-care toolkit to use after boundary breaches. Include items and activities that help you relax, recharge, and regain your emotional balance. This might include books, music, bath products, mindfulness exercises, or contact information for supportive friends.

4. Visualization Exercise for Boundary Maintenance

   - Visualize a challenging situation where you successfully maintain your boundaries. Picture yourself responding calmly and assertively, and imagine the positive outcome. Repeat this exercise regularly to reinforce your confidence and preparedness.

Conclusion

Maintaining boundaries is an ongoing process that requires consistency, clear communication, and self-care. By regularly reinforcing your boundaries and addressing violations effectively, you can protect your well-being and enhance your relationships. The strategies, prompts, and exercises in this chapter provide practical tools to help you uphold your boundaries confidently and consistently. As you continue your journey, remember that boundary maintenance is a dynamic process that evolves with your needs and experiences. Stay committed to your self-care and growth, and recognize that each step you take strengthens your ability to live authentically and empowered.

ENTER YOUR JOURNAL HERE

CHAPTER 5: COMMUNICATING BOUNDARIES EFFECTIVELY

Effective communication is vital for establishing and maintaining healthy boundaries. How you express your needs and limits can significantly impact whether others respect them. This chapter explores the principles and techniques of assertive communication, how to handle difficult conversations, and the importance of non-verbal cues in boundary setting.

Subtopic 1: Principles of Assertive Communication

Understanding Assertiveness

Assertiveness is the ability to express your thoughts, feelings, and needs directly, honestly, and respectfully. It stands in contrast to passive, aggressive, or passive-aggressive communication styles.

- Passive Communication: Involves avoiding the expression of one's needs, often leading to feelings of resentment and frustration.

- Aggressive Communication: Involves expressing needs in a forceful and hostile manner, which can alienate others.

- Passive-Aggressive Communication: Involves expressing needs indirectly or through manipulation, often leading to misunderstandings and conflicts.

Assertive communication respects both your own needs and the needs of others, fostering healthy and respectful interactions.

Key Components of Assertive Communication

1. Clarity: Be clear and specific about your needs and boundaries. Avoid vague statements that can be misinterpreted.

2. Confidence: Speak with confidence, maintaining a steady tone and eye contact. This conveys that you are serious about your boundaries.

3. Respect: Show respect for the other person's feelings and perspective. Use polite language and listen actively.

4. Calmness: Maintain a calm demeanor, even in challenging conversations. This helps prevent escalation and keeps the discussion productive.

Subtopic 2: Techniques for Effective Communication

Using "I" Statements

"I" statements focus on your own feelings and needs rather than blaming or criticizing others. This reduces defensiveness and encourages constructive dialogue.

- Example: "I feel overwhelmed when I am interrupted during work. I need uninterrupted time to concentrate."

Active Listening

Active listening involves fully concentrating on what the other person is saying, understanding their message, and responding thoughtfully. It demonstrates respect and openness to finding a mutually acceptable solution.

- Techniques:
  - Paraphrasing: Restate what the other person has said to ensure understanding.

- Reflecting: Reflect on the emotions behind their words.

- Clarifying: Ask questions if something is unclear.

Setting and Reinforcing Boundaries

1. Initial Boundary Setting: Clearly state your boundary the first time you communicate it.

  - Example: "I need to leave work by 6 PM to spend time with my family."

2. Reinforcement: If the boundary is crossed, reinforce it by restating your needs and the importance of the boundary.

  - Example: "I understand this project is important, but I must leave by 6 PM as planned. Can we discuss a way to manage this within my working hours?"

3. Setting Consequences: Clearly outline the consequences if the boundary continues to be violated.

- Example: "If I continue to be asked to stay late, I will need to discuss adjusting my workload."

Subtopic 3: Handling Difficult Conversations

Preparing for the Conversation

1. Plan Ahead: Think about what you want to say and how you will say it. Anticipate possible reactions and prepare your responses.

2. Choose the Right Time and Place: Find a private, calm setting where you can talk without interruptions.

3. Stay Focused: Keep the conversation focused on the specific boundary and avoid bringing up unrelated issues.

Managing Emotional Reactions

1. Stay Calm: Practice deep breathing or mindfulness techniques to stay calm during the conversation.

2. Acknowledge Emotions: Recognize and validate both your own emotions and those of the other person.

- Example: "I understand this is frustrating, and I feel the same way."

Finding Common Ground

1. Seek Solutions Together: Engage the other person in finding a solution that respects both your boundary and their needs.

   - Example: "Can we agree on a schedule that allows me to leave by 6 PM while still meeting our project deadlines?"

2. Compromise When Possible: Be open to compromise while still maintaining the core of your boundary.

   - Example: "I can adjust my hours slightly during peak project times, but I need advance notice."

Subtopic 4: Non-Verbal Communication

The Role of Non-Verbal Cues

Non-verbal communication, including body language, facial expressions, and tone of voice, plays a significant role in how your boundaries are perceived. Consistent non-verbal cues reinforce your verbal messages and demonstrate confidence.

Key Non-Verbal Techniques

1. Maintain Eye Contact: Shows confidence and sincerity.

2. Use Open Body Language: Stand or sit with an open posture to show openness and assertiveness.

3. Steady Tone of Voice: Speak in a clear, steady tone to convey confidence and seriousness.

4. Facial Expressions: Ensure your facial expressions match your verbal message. A serious expression when discussing important boundaries emphasizes your commitment.

Prompts and Exercises for Chapter 5

Prompts

1. "Write about a time when you had to communicate a difficult boundary. How did you approach it, and what was the outcome?"

   - Reflect on a challenging boundary-setting experience. Consider what worked well and what could be improved for future conversations.

2. "Describe a situation where you felt your boundary was not respected. How did you communicate your needs, and what could you have done differently?"

   - Analyze a past experience to identify areas for improvement in your communication strategy.

3. "What are three boundaries you find difficult to communicate? Why do you find them challenging, and how can you approach these conversations more effectively?"

   - Identify challenging boundaries and brainstorm strategies to communicate them more effectively.

Exercises

1. Assertive Communication Practice

   - Practice assertive communication techniques with a friend or in front of a mirror. Focus on using "I" statements, maintaining eye contact, and using a steady tone of voice.

2. Role-Playing Difficult Conversations

   - Role-play difficult boundary-setting conversations with a trusted friend or family member. Take turns playing different roles and providing feedback on each other's communication techniques.

3. Non-Verbal Communication Exercise

   - Record yourself practicing boundary-setting statements. Pay attention to your body language, facial expressions, and tone of voice. Review the recording to identify areas for improvement.

4. Active Listening Practice

- Pair up with a friend or family member and practice active listening techniques. Take turns speaking and actively listening, using paraphrasing, reflecting, and clarifying questions to ensure understanding.

Conclusion

Effective communication is the cornerstone of setting and maintaining healthy boundaries. By mastering assertive communication techniques, handling difficult conversations with confidence, and utilizing non-verbal cues effectively, you can ensure that your boundaries are respected and upheld. The strategies, prompts, and exercises in this chapter provide practical tools to enhance your communication skills and strengthen your ability to live authentically and empowered. As you continue your journey, remember that effective communication is a skill that can be developed and refined over time, leading to healthier relationships and a more fulfilling life.

ENTER YOUR JOURNAL HERE

Chapter 6: Boundaries in Different Contexts

Boundaries are essential across various areas of life, including personal relationships, professional settings, and digital spaces. This chapter explores how to adapt and apply boundary-setting principles to different contexts, offering tailored strategies and examples for maintaining healthy boundaries in each area.

Subtopic 1: Personal Relationships

Boundaries with Family

Family relationships often come with deep emotional ties and longstanding patterns, making boundary-setting both crucial and challenging.

1. Identify Specific Needs: Recognize areas where you need boundaries, such as personal space, privacy, and emotional support.

   - Example: "I need time alone after family gatherings to recharge."

2. Communicate Clearly: Use direct, respectful communication to express your needs.

- Example: "I appreciate your concern, but I need to make my own decisions about my career."

3. Set Limits on Emotional Labor: Establish boundaries around the emotional support you provide.

   - Example: "I can listen to your concerns, but I can't be available for late-night calls every day."

4. Establish Physical Space Boundaries: Define and respect physical boundaries within shared living spaces.

   - Example: "Please knock before entering my room."

Boundaries with Friends

Healthy friendships require mutual respect and understanding of each other's boundaries.

1. Balance Giving and Receiving: Ensure that the friendship is reciprocal in terms of emotional and practical support.

   - Example: "I enjoy helping you, but I also need support sometimes."

2. Set Time Boundaries: Protect your time to prevent overcommitment.

   - Example: "I can hang out this weekend, but I need to leave by 8 PM to get enough rest."

3. Communicate Comfort Levels: Be open about what you are comfortable with in social settings.

   - Example: "I prefer quieter gatherings rather than large parties."

Boundaries with Romantic Partners

Boundaries in romantic relationships are vital for maintaining individual identities and a healthy dynamic.

1. Maintain Individuality: Preserve your own interests and time apart from the relationship.

   - Example: "I need a night each week to spend time with my hobbies."

2. Set Expectations for Communication: Define how and when you will communicate, especially during conflicts.

   - Example: "Let's agree to take a break and cool off before discussing heated topics."

3. Respect Personal Space: Ensure each partner has their own space and privacy.

   - Example: "I need some alone time each day to unwind."

4. Discuss Financial Boundaries: Clearly outline how you handle finances within the relationship.

   - Example: "We should each contribute to shared expenses but maintain separate accounts for personal spending."

Subtopic 2: Professional Boundaries

Boundaries with Colleagues

Maintaining professional boundaries with colleagues promotes a respectful and productive work environment.

1. Define Work Hours: Clearly communicate your working hours and availability.

   - Example: "I am available for work-related calls between 9 AM and 5 PM."

2. Set Limits on Personal Sharing: Decide how much personal information you are comfortable sharing at work.

   - Example: "I prefer to keep my personal life separate from my professional life."

3. Respect Workspace Boundaries: Honor each other's physical workspace and privacy.

   - Example: "Please knock before entering my office."

4. Address Conflicts Professionally: Handle disagreements with respect and professionalism.

   - Example: "Let's discuss this issue calmly and find a solution together."

Boundaries with Supervisors

Establishing boundaries with supervisors is essential for maintaining a healthy work-life balance and professional respect.

1. Clarify Job Expectations: Ensure your job role and responsibilities are clearly defined.

   - Example: "Can we review my job description to clarify my duties?"

2. Set Communication Norms: Agree on appropriate times and methods for communication.

- Example: "I am available for urgent matters via phone after hours, but non-urgent issues can wait until the next workday."

3. Protect Personal Time: Advocate for your right to personal time and avoid overworking.

- Example: "I need to leave on time to manage my work-life balance effectively."

4. Seek Support When Needed: Don't hesitate to request support or resources when necessary.

- Example: "I need additional resources to complete this project on time."

Subtopic 3: Digital Boundaries

Social Media Boundaries

Social media can blur the lines between public and private life, making boundary-setting essential.

1. Control Privacy Settings: Adjust your privacy settings to control who can see your posts and personal information.

  - Example: "I keep my social media profiles private to protect my personal information."

2. Limit Screen Time: Set boundaries on how much time you spend on social media.

  - Example: "I limit my social media use to 30 minutes per day to avoid distractions."

3. Be Mindful of Sharing: Consider the impact of what you share and avoid oversharing personal details.

  - Example: "I avoid posting about my personal struggles on social media."

4. Manage Interactions: Decide how and when you will interact with others online.

- Example: "I do not engage in political debates on social media to maintain my mental peace."

Work-Related Digital Boundaries

With the rise of remote work, maintaining digital boundaries in professional settings is crucial.

1. Set Email Boundaries: Define when you will check and respond to work emails.

 - Example: "I check emails twice a day and do not respond to work emails after 6 PM."

2. Use Separate Devices: If possible, use separate devices for work and personal use to delineate boundaries.

 - Example: "I use a work laptop for office tasks and a personal computer for other activities."

3. Communicate Availability: Clearly state your availability for virtual meetings and work-related communications.

   - Example: "I am available for meetings between 9 AM and 4 PM."

4. Respect Others' Digital Boundaries: Be mindful of your colleagues' digital boundaries and communication preferences.

   - Example: "I respect my colleagues' out-of-office messages and do not expect immediate responses."

Prompts and Exercises for Chapter 6

Prompts

1. "Reflect on a personal relationship where setting a boundary was challenging. What was the situation, and how did you handle it?"

- Analyze a difficult boundary-setting scenario in a personal relationship to identify what you did well and what could be improved.

2. "Write about a time when your professional boundaries were not respected. How did you address the situation?"

- Consider a professional boundary breach and evaluate your response to develop better strategies for the future.

3. "Describe your current digital boundaries. How do you manage your time and interactions online, and what changes could improve your digital well-being?"

- Reflect on your digital habits and boundaries, identifying areas for improvement to enhance your online experience.

Exercises

1. Personal Boundaries Action Plan

- Create a detailed action plan for setting and maintaining boundaries in your personal relationships. Include specific strategies for different relationships, such as family, friends, and romantic partners.

2. Professional Boundaries Worksheet

   - Develop a worksheet to outline your professional boundaries. Include sections for work hours, communication norms, and handling conflicts. Review and adjust the worksheet as needed to ensure it remains effective.

3. Digital Detox Challenge

   - Commit to a digital detox challenge for a specified period, such as a weekend or a week. Limit your use of social media and work-related digital interactions. Reflect on how the detox affects your well-being and productivity.

4. Role-Playing Boundary Scenarios

- Partner with a friend or colleague to role-play boundary-setting scenarios in different contexts. Practice handling challenging conversations and reinforcing your boundaries with confidence and respect.

Conclusion

Boundaries are crucial across all areas of life, from personal relationships to professional settings and digital spaces. Adapting boundary-setting principles to different contexts requires clear communication, self-awareness, and consistent.

ENTER YOUR JOURNAL HERE

....

....

....

....

....

....

....

....

....

....

....

....

....

....

....

CHAPTER 6: BOUNDARIES IN DIFFERENT CONTEXTS

Boundaries play a critical role in our well-being and interactions, and their application varies across different contexts. This chapter delves into the nuances of setting and maintaining boundaries in personal relationships, professional environments, and digital spaces. Understanding these distinctions helps ensure that boundaries are respected and upheld in every aspect of life.

Subtopic 1: Personal Relationships

Boundaries with Family

Family dynamics often come with deep-rooted patterns and expectations, making boundary-setting both essential and challenging. Here's how to navigate this terrain effectively:

1. Identifying Needs: Recognize where you need boundaries to protect your well-being. Common areas include privacy, emotional support, and time management.

   - Example: "I need alone time after family gatherings to recharge."

2. Communicating Clearly: Use straightforward, respectful language to express your boundaries.

   - Example: "I appreciate your concern, but I need to make my own decisions about my career."

3. Managing Emotional Labor: Set limits on the emotional support you provide to prevent burnout.

   - Example: "I can listen to your concerns, but I need to set limits on late-night calls."

4. Establishing Physical Space Boundaries: Clearly define and respect personal spaces within the home.

   - Example: "Please knock before entering my room."

Boundaries with Friends

Healthy friendships are built on mutual respect and understanding of each other's boundaries. Here's how to maintain them:

1. Balancing Support: Ensure the friendship is reciprocal in terms of giving and receiving support.

- Example: "I enjoy helping you, but I also need support sometimes."

2. Setting Time Boundaries: Protect your time to prevent overcommitment and burnout.

  - Example: "I can hang out this weekend, but I need to leave by 8 PM to rest."

3. Communicating Comfort Levels: Be open about your comfort zones in social settings.

  - Example: "I prefer quieter gatherings rather than large parties."

4. Addressing Conflicts: Resolve conflicts respectfully and directly to maintain trust and respect.

  - Example: "I felt hurt when you canceled our plans last minute. Can we discuss how to prevent this in the future?"

Boundaries with Romantic Partners

Boundaries in romantic relationships are vital for maintaining individual identities and fostering a healthy partnership.

1. Maintaining Individuality: Preserve your own interests and personal time apart from the relationship.

   - Example: "I need a night each week to spend time on my hobbies."

2. Setting Communication Expectations: Define how and when to communicate, especially during conflicts.

   - Example: "Let's agree to take a break and cool off before discussing heated topics."

3. Respecting Personal Space: Ensure each partner has their own space and privacy.

   - Example: "I need some alone time each day to unwind."

4. Discussing Financial Boundaries: Clearly outline how finances will be managed within the relationship.

   - Example: "We should each contribute to shared expenses but maintain separate accounts for personal spending."

Subtopic 2: Professional Boundaries

Boundaries with Colleagues

Maintaining professional boundaries with colleagues promotes a respectful and productive work environment.

1. Defining Work Hours: Clearly communicate your working hours and availability.

   - Example: "I am available for work-related calls between 9 AM and 5 PM."

2. Limiting Personal Sharing: Decide how much personal information you are comfortable sharing at work.

   - Example: "I prefer to keep my personal life separate from my professional life."

3. Respecting Workspace Boundaries: Honor each other's physical workspace and privacy.

   - Example: "Please knock before entering my office."

4. Handling Conflicts Professionally: Address disagreements with respect and professionalism.

   - Example: "Let's discuss this issue calmly and find a solution together."

Boundaries with Supervisors

Establishing boundaries with supervisors is essential for maintaining a healthy work-life balance and professional respect.

1. Clarifying Job Expectations: Ensure your job role and responsibilities are clearly defined.

   - Example: "Can we review my job description to clarify my duties?"

2. Setting Communication Norms: Agree on appropriate times and methods for communication.

   - Example: "I am available for urgent matters via phone after hours, but non-urgent issues can wait until the next workday."

3. Protecting Personal Time: Advocate for your right to personal time and avoid overworking.

   - Example: "I need to leave on time to manage my work-life balance effectively."

4. Seeking Support When Needed: Don't hesitate to request support or resources when necessary.

   - Example: "I need additional resources to complete this project on time."

Subtopic 3: Digital Boundaries

Social Media Boundaries

Social media can blur the lines between public and private life, making boundary-setting essential.

1. Controlling Privacy Settings: Adjust your privacy settings to control who can see your posts and personal information.

 - Example: "I keep my social media profiles private to protect my personal information."

2. Limiting Screen Time: Set boundaries on how much time you spend on social media.

 - Example: "I limit my social media use to 30 minutes per day to avoid distractions."

3. Being Mindful of Sharing: Consider the impact of what you share and avoid oversharing personal details.

 - Example: "I avoid posting about my personal struggles on social media."

4. Managing Interactions: Decide how and when you will interact with others online.

   - Example: "I do not engage in political debates on social media to maintain my mental peace."

Work-Related Digital Boundaries

With the rise of remote work, maintaining digital boundaries in professional settings is crucial.

1. Setting Email Boundaries: Define when you will check and respond to work emails.

   - Example: "I check emails twice a day and do not respond to work emails after 6 PM."

2. Using Separate Devices: If possible, use separate devices for work and personal use to delineate boundaries.

- Example: "I use a work laptop for office tasks and a personal computer for other activities."

3. Communicating Availability: Clearly state your availability for virtual meetings and work-related communications.

   - Example: "I am available for meetings between 9 AM and 4 PM."

4. Respecting Others' Digital Boundaries: Be mindful of your colleagues' digital boundaries and communication preferences.

   - Example: "I respect my colleagues' out-of-office messages and do not expect immediate responses."

Prompts and Exercises for Chapter 6

Prompts

1. "Reflect on a personal relationship where setting a boundary was challenging. What was the situation, and how did you handle it?"

- Analyze a difficult boundary-setting scenario in a personal relationship to identify what you did well and what could be improved.

2. "Write about a time when your professional boundaries were not respected. How did you address the situation?"

 - Consider a professional boundary breach and evaluate your response to develop better strategies for the future.

3. "Describe your current digital boundaries. How do you manage your time and interactions online, and what changes could improve your digital well-being?"

 - Reflect on your digital habits and boundaries, identifying areas for improvement to enhance your online experience.

Exercises

1. Personal Boundaries Action Plan

- Create a detailed action plan for setting and maintaining boundaries in your personal relationships. Include specific strategies for different relationships, such as family, friends, and romantic partners.

2. Professional Boundaries Worksheet

  - Develop a worksheet to outline your professional boundaries. Include sections for work hours, communication norms, and handling conflicts. Review and adjust the worksheet as needed to ensure it remains effective.

3. Digital Detox Challenge

  - Commit to a digital detox challenge for a specified period, such as a weekend or a week. Limit your use of social media and work-related digital interactions. Reflect on how the detox affects your well-being and productivity.

4. Role-Playing Boundary Scenarios

- Partner with a friend or colleague to role-play boundary-setting scenarios in different contexts. Practice handling challenging conversations and reinforcing your boundaries with confidence and respect.

Conclusion

Boundaries are crucial across all areas of life, from personal relationships to professional settings and digital spaces. Adapting boundary-setting principles to different contexts requires clear communication, self-awareness, and consistent reinforcement. The strategies, prompts, and exercises in this chapter provide practical tools to help you establish and maintain healthy boundaries in various areas of your life. As you continue your journey, remember that boundary-setting is an ongoing process that evolves with your needs and experiences. Stay committed to your self-care and growth, and recognize that each step you take strengthens your ability to live authentically and empowered.

ENTER YOUR JOURNAL HERE

....

....

....

....

....

....

....

CHAPTER 7: OVERCOMING BOUNDARY VIOLATIONS

Boundary violations can be deeply unsettling, often leading to feelings of frustration, anger, and helplessness. Learning to handle these violations effectively is crucial for maintaining your sense of self and ensuring your boundaries are respected in the future. This chapter focuses on understanding boundary violations, responding to them assertively, and healing from their impact.

Subtopic 1: Understanding Boundary Violations

Types of Boundary Violations

Boundary violations can take many forms, depending on the context and relationship. Understanding these different types can help you identify and address them effectively:

1. Physical Violations: Intruding into your personal space without consent.

   - Example: Someone standing too close to you, touching you without permission, or entering your room without knocking.

2. Emotional Violations: Disregarding your feelings and emotional well-being.

   - Example: A friend belittling your feelings, or a partner ignoring your emotional needs.

3. Material Violations: Using or taking your possessions without permission.

   - Example: A colleague borrowing your items without asking, or a family member using your car without informing you.

4. Intellectual Violations: Dismissing or mocking your ideas and opinions.

   - Example: A colleague interrupting and disregarding your contributions in meetings, or a friend making fun of your beliefs.

5. Time Violations: Disregarding your time and personal schedule.

   - Example: Someone consistently arriving late, asking you to work overtime without prior notice, or expecting immediate responses to messages.

Recognizing Boundary Violations

Being aware of the signs of boundary violations is the first step toward addressing them. Common indicators include:

1. Discomfort and Unease: Feeling uneasy or uncomfortable during interactions.

2. Resentment and Anger: Experiencing growing resentment or anger towards someone.

3. Feeling Drained: Noticing a pattern of feeling emotionally or physically drained after interactions.

4. Compromised Values: Realizing you are compromising your values and needs to accommodate others.

Subtopic 2: Responding to Boundary Violations

Immediate Responses

When a boundary violation occurs, your immediate response can set the tone for how future interactions unfold. Here are some strategies for responding effectively:

1. Stay Calm: Take a moment to breathe and compose yourself before responding. This helps prevent an emotional reaction that might escalate the situation.

- Example: If someone interrupts you repeatedly, take a deep breath before addressing it.

2. Use Assertive Communication: Clearly and respectfully communicate your boundary and the violation.

- Example: "I feel uncomfortable when my personal space is invaded. Please respect my need for personal space."

3. Set Immediate Consequences: If appropriate, outline the immediate consequence of the boundary violation.

- Example: "If you continue to interrupt me, I will end this conversation."

Reinforcing Boundaries

Consistently reinforcing your boundaries is essential for ensuring they are respected over time. Here are some strategies to reinforce your boundaries:

1. Restate Your Boundary: Reiterate your boundary if it continues to be violated.

   - Example: "I've mentioned before that I need my alone time after work. Please respect that."

2. Be Consistent: Consistency is key to maintaining boundaries. Apply the same boundary and consequences every time.

   - Example: If you have a rule about not working on weekends, consistently decline work-related requests during that time.

3. Follow Through with Consequences: Ensure that the consequences you set are enforced if the boundary is violated again.

   - Example: If a friend repeatedly borrows items without asking, you might say, "I won't be able to lend you things anymore because you haven't asked for my permission."

Seeking Support

Sometimes, handling boundary violations can be challenging, and seeking support from others can be beneficial:

1. Talk to a Trusted Friend: Share your experience with someone you trust to gain perspective and advice.

   - Example: Discussing a colleague's behavior with a friend who understands your professional environment.

2. Seek Professional Help: A therapist or counselor can provide strategies and support for dealing with persistent boundary violations.

   - Example: If family members continually disregard your boundaries, a therapist can help you navigate these complex dynamics.

3. Join Support Groups: Connecting with others who have faced similar issues can provide validation and practical advice.

   - Example: Joining a support group for workplace harassment victims can offer strategies for dealing with boundary violations at work.

Subtopic 3: Healing from Boundary Violations

Emotional Healing

Boundary violations can leave emotional scars that require healing. Here are steps to facilitate emotional recovery:

1. Acknowledge Your Feelings: Allow yourself to fully feel and acknowledge the emotions resulting from the violation.

    - Example: Writing in a journal about your feelings can help process them.

2. Practice Self-Compassion: Be kind to yourself and recognize that setting and maintaining boundaries is a learning process.

    - Example: Remind yourself that it's okay to make mistakes and that you're doing your best.

3. Engage in Self-Care: Prioritize activities that nourish your mind, body, and spirit.

- Example: Regular exercise, meditation, and spending time with loved ones can help restore your emotional well-being.

Rebuilding Trust

If a boundary violation has damaged trust in a relationship, rebuilding that trust is a gradual process:

1. Open Communication: Have an honest conversation with the person who violated your boundary.

   - Example: "I feel hurt by what happened, and I need to talk about how we can prevent this in the future."

2. Set Clear Expectations: Clearly outline what you need moving forward to rebuild trust.

   - Example: "For us to rebuild trust, I need you to respect my personal space and ask for permission before borrowing my things."

3. Give It Time: Understand that rebuilding trust takes time and requires consistent effort from both parties.

   - Example: Gradually re-establishing boundaries and monitoring the other person's behavior over time.

Learning and Growing

Every boundary violation can be a learning opportunity that strengthens your future boundary-setting skills:

1. Reflect on the Experience: Consider what you've learned from the violation and how it can inform your future boundary-setting efforts.

   - Example: "I've learned that I need to be more assertive and clear about my boundaries from the beginning."

2. Adjust Your Boundaries: Based on your reflections, adjust your boundaries as needed to better protect your well-being.

   - Example: Implementing a more rigid boundary around your personal time to prevent future violations.

3. Empower Yourself: Use the experience to empower yourself and build confidence in your ability to set and maintain boundaries.

   - Example: Acknowledging your growth and resilience in handling boundary violations can boost your self-esteem and assertiveness.

Prompts and Exercises for Chapter 7

Prompts

1. "Describe a time when your boundary was violated. How did you respond, and what was the outcome?"

   - Reflect on a specific incident to analyze your response and its effectiveness, identifying areas for improvement.

2. "Write about your feelings and emotions when someone violates your boundaries. How do these experiences affect your overall well-being?"

   - Explore the emotional impact of boundary violations to better understand their effects and your emotional responses.

3. "Think of a boundary violation that you handled successfully. What steps did you take, and why do you think they were effective?"

   - Identify a positive experience to reinforce effective strategies and build confidence in your ability to manage future violations.

Exercises

1. Boundary Violation Role-Playing

   - Partner with a friend or colleague to role-play scenarios where boundaries are violated. Practice responding assertively and reinforcing your boundaries.

2. Emotional Processing Journal

- Keep a journal specifically for processing emotions related to boundary violations. Write about your feelings, responses, and lessons learned from each incident.

3. Self-Care Action Plan

  - Create a detailed self-care plan to implement after experiencing a boundary violation. Include activities that promote emotional healing and well-being.

4. Trust Rebuilding Checklist

  - Develop a checklist for rebuilding trust in relationships after a boundary violation. Include steps for open communication, setting expectations, and monitoring progress.

Conclusion

Boundary violations are an inevitable part of life, but how you respond to them can significantly impact your well-being and relationships. By understanding different types of violations, responding assertively, and engaging in healing practices, you can protect your boundaries and strengthen your resilience. The strategies, prompts, and exercises in this chapter provide practical tools to help you navigate and overcome boundary violations. As you continue your journey, remember that each experience, no matter how challenging, is an opportunity for growth and empowerment. Stay committed to your self-care and boundary-setting efforts, knowing that you have the strength and capability to live authentically and empowered.

ENTER YOUR JOURNAL HERE

....

....

....

....

....

Printed in Great Britain
by Amazon